Living with

SELF-HARM BEHAVIOURS

DR ONG SAY HOW

Marshall Cavendish
Editions

© 2015 Marshall Cavendish International (Asia) Private Limited

Illustrations by Julie Davey
Series designer: Bernard Go

First published 2003 by Times Editions

This 2015 edition published by
Marshall Cavendish Editions
An imprint of Marshall Cavendish International
1 New Industrial Road, Singapore 536196

Other Marshall Cavendish Offices
Marshall Cavendish Corporation. 99 White Plains Road, Tarrytown NY 10591-9001, USA • Marshall
Cavendish International (Thailand) Co Ltd. 253 Asoke, 12th Flr, Sukhumvit 21 Road, Klongtoey Nua,
Wattana, Bangkok 10110, Thailand • Marshall Cavendish (Malaysia) Sdn Bhd, Times Subang, Lot 46,
Subang Hi-Tech Industrial Park, Batu Tiga, 40000 Shah Alam, Selangor Darul Ehsan, Malaysia

Marshall Cavendish is a trademark of Times Publishing Limited.

National Library Board, Singapore Cataloguing-in-Publication Data
Ong, Say How, author.
Living with self-harm behaviours / Dr Ong Say How; illustrations by Julie Davey.
– Singapore: Marshall Cavendish Editions, 2015.
pages cm
ISBN: 978-981-4634-22-9 (paperback)

1. Self-destructive behavior – Popular works. 2. Self-destructive behavior in children.
3. Self-destructive behavior in adolescence. 4. Children – Suicidal behavior. 5. Teenagers –
Suicidal behavior. I. Davey, Julie, illustrator. II. Title. III. Living with.

RJ506.S39
616.858200835 — dc23   OCN912354895

Printed in Singapore by Markono Print Media Pte Ltd

Dedicated to
all my patients and children of Child Guidance Clinic
and their parents

CONTENTS

PREFACE

Self-harm behaviour is not uncommon in all communities and strikes people from all walks of life. It is often not spoken about because it arouses negative feelings of shame, guilt and remorse, particularly in Asian societies where it is considered taboo to talk of one's private affairs publicly. Sufferers who speak up may be ostracised and seen as weak and useless. So their plight is not known to many.

Self-harm behaviours cannot be easily wished away and should not go unnoticed. The fact that children and teenagers engage in self-harm behaviours definitely raises concerns. Why should people in the prime of their youth want to hurt themselves?

It must be recognised that young people may not necessarily have the means and resources to cope with their emotional problems. Many do not dare to turn to their parents or teachers for help. If our society does not protect and help them, then who will?

This book aims to present the facts behind self-harm behaviours for parents, teachers, counsellors and anyone who interacts with children and teenagers. This new edition also provides updates on self-harm, including recent local statistics and new community-based resources, such as REACH and CHAT, that could help young persons who experience self-harm.

I would like to thank my fellow colleagues at the Child Guidance Clinic for encouraging me to complete this book.

Dr Ong Say How
July 2015

INTRODUCTION

❝ I came to the hospital's A&E so often that one of the nurses told me I was a pain in the neck for having to keep coming in. ❞
— Angela, 18 years old

❝ The hospital staff thinks that treating us is a waste of time because they should be treating people who truly want to get better and don't deliberately hurt themselves. ❞
— Chris, 17 years old

People who intentionally harm themselves are often ostracised in society as the reasons for them doing so are poorly understood, even as we continue to learn more about them and their self-destructive behaviours. Self-harm behaviours are baffling for caregivers who cannot understand why young persons would want to harm themselves and if so, why they do so repeatedly. Parents are dumbfounded and often give up after failing to obtain any answers from their children.

These young persons may also be shunned by their friends and peers, as well as by the medical personnel who attend to them when they seek treatment at hospitals.

Self-harm behaviours can afflict both teens and even young children below 12 years old, although the occurrence in the latter age group is much lower. In this book, "young persons" is used to refer to youths between the ages of 12 and 18 years old.

Just what is self-harm? Why do youngsters harm themselves and what can we do about it? This book attempts to explain this phenomenon, offer new insights and suggestions on what families and schools can do to reduce its occurrence. By trying to understand individuals who self-harm, we will hopefully effect a change in them and not relegate them to the fringes of society.

WHAT IS SELF-HARM?

PART 1

Self-harm describes a wide range of acts that people deliberately do to hurt or injure themselves. A more accurate term for self-harm is Non-Suicidal Self-Injury (NSSI), which is defined as "the deliberate, direct and self-inflicted destruction of body tissue resulting in immediate tissue damage, for purposes not socially sanctioned and without suicidal intent" by the International Society for the Study of Self-Injury. For simplicity, the terms "self-harm" and "non-suicidal self-injury" are used interchangeably in this book.

Individuals who engage in self-harm behaviours are in great emotional turmoil. Most self-harmers feel very alone as they believe they have become different from normal people and have no one to trust or share their problems with. They have conspicuous scars on their limbs which cannot be easily explained away, and which they conceal with bandages or long-sleeved shirts.

The seriousness of the problem is not measured by how bad or how extensive the injury is. People who hurt themselves a little can be feeling just as bad as those who hurt themselves a lot. Many self-harmers hurt themselves secretly for a long time before they eventually find the courage to tell someone about it or come forward for help.

1.1 WHAT ARE THE COMMON METHODS THAT PEOPLE USE TO HARM THEMSELVES?

In Singapore, most cases of self-harm are caused by inflicting superficial cuts on the wrists and forearms with penknives and other sharp objects (knives, razors, broken glass, metal rulers and pins). Some common methods are:

- cutting or carving on skin,
- scratching or biting skin,
- burning skin,
- pulling hair out,
- peeling skin until it bleeds,
- picking on an old wound so that it does not heal,
- hitting one's body with an object or punching oneself,
- hitting or banging self against walls or other hard objects,
- embedding foreign objects under the skin,
- overdosing with medications or drugs (self-poisoning).

Self-harm by drug overdose is a relatively common method used here. The most commonly used drugs are the ones that are readily available like Paracetamol (commonly known as Panadol) and minor tranquillisers such as sleeping pills and relaxants. Overdosing does not usually endanger life unless the dosage is so massive such that the drug causes liver failure or other complications in the central nervous system.

As one of the criteria for self-harm must be that its purpose is not socially sanctioned, tattooing and body piercing would not have technically been constituted as self-harm behaviour unless they are carried to the extreme. Likewise, other potentially harmful behaviours like smoking and alcohol intake are not typically regarded as self-harm although they could cause negative health effects. Substance abuse (e.g. glue-sniffing and illicit drug use) and eating disorders (e.g. anorexia nervosa and bulimia nervosa) may be regarded by some to be forms of self-harm, but the purposes for these behaviours are very different, warranting separate diagnostic classification, assessment and management. These are hence not included for discussion in this book.

Whatever the nature of the act, self-harm is always a sign that something has gone seriously wrong.

1.2   HOW COMMON IS SELF-HARM AMONG CHILDREN AND YOUNG PERSONS?

Self-harm by children and young people is not uncommon, even in Singapore. It is difficult to give a true estimate of just how many children and young people engage in self-harm acts here as such acts are often done in private. What we see at the clinics is just tip of the iceberg. Some mental health professionals say as many as one in ten teenagers could be affected. The number of cases actually seen by medical personnel is probably fewer as only the reported or severe cases are treated. In the US, it is estimated that about 1 per cent of the population self-harm. In the UK, the British government estimates that one in seventeen adolescents are self-harming.

In general, studies suggest that about 13 per cent to 25 per cent of adolescents and young adults surveyed in schools have some history of self-harm behaviours (Rodham & Hawton, 2009). There is no age limit as to when self-harm can occur, but students in secondary schools have somewhat higher prevalence as the average age of onset for self-harm tends to occur at 14 to 16 years.

1.3 DO PEOPLE WHO SELF-HARM HURT THEMSELVES REPEATEDLY?

While many who self-harm did so only once or twice and then stopped, others become chronic self injurers. This demographic profile seems to be similar worldwide. Studies conducted overseas revealed that:

- approximately 20 per cent to 30 per cent of young persons seen at hospitals had engaged in previous acts of self-harm,
- between 10 per cent and 15 per cent of self-harmers carried out a further act within the following year.

Repeated acts of self-harm indicate that these individuals face persistent or recurrent psychosocial problems. More importantly, they are associated with a considerable risk of actual completed suicide.

1.4 WHO ARE THE PEOPLE WHO ARE LIKELY TO HARM THEMSELVES?

A study by Ho & Kua (1998) revealed interesting data about self-harmers in Singapore. Of 814 patients admitted to the National University Hospital, they found that:

- women (60.5 per cent) were more likely to harm themselves than men,
- the female to male ratio was 7:1,
- the behaviour began in the teen years and continued into the late twenties and early thirties,
- self-harmers usually come from the middle or upper socio-economic classes,
- self-harmers are intelligent and well educated.

However, self-harm is seen across all cultures, races and religious groups. The risk increases if the person comes from a background of physical and/or sexual abuse or has at least one alcoholic parent. People who self-harm may also suffer from eating disorders.

1.5 WHY ARE WOMEN MORE LIKELY TO HARM THEMSELVES THAN MEN?

It is quite clear that women tend to resort to self-harm behaviours more often than men. In 1994, Dusty Miller, a training director and author of the book, *Women Who Hurt Themselves*, postulated that women are socialised to internalise anger and men to externalise it.

Men are socialised to repress emotion by putting on a stoic and brave facade, or externalise it in seemingly unrelated acts of violence. This means that when overwhelmed by distressing or negative emotions, men have a choice to act out in behaviours such as drinking, fighting or vandalising property. In contrast, women are not socialised to express violence externally and when confronted with unpleasant or depressive emotions, will tend to vent that rage on themselves.

1.6   IS SELF-HARM DANGEROUS OR LIFE-THREATENING?

Most self-harm acts appear to be harmful but they are usually not dangerous and they do not kill. However, death or permanent injury may result even if it was not the intention. Accidents can happen and precious lives are lost. For years, there have been media reports of famous people or celebrities who accidentally killed themselves by a drug overdose. Their initial intention was perhaps to escape from daily pressures in the entertainment or political circles.

1.7   WHAT IS THE RELATIONSHIP BETWEEN SELF-HARM AND SUICIDE?

The relationship between self-harm and suicide is complex. Many people who have harmed themselves have harboured thoughts of suicide at some point in time. We should remember, though, that self-harm in itself is not failed suicide. Most self-harm acts also do not include attempted suicide or injury that is incidental to another activity.

For the purpose of clarity, self-harm is regarded as a separate entity and distinct from intended suicide. This is because the motivation behind the two acts is very different. Even then, a case of serious, repeated self-harm acts may progress into suicide eventually. Suicide is more serious as the person would have decided, after much pondering, to end his life to escape from his problems permanently. Part 6 of this book discusses this relationship in greater detail.

1.8   TO WHAT EXTENT DOES PERSONALITY AND TEMPERAMENT PREDISPOSE A PERSON TO SELF-HARM BEHAVIOUR?

There are many postulations and theories about the relationship between a person's temperament and self-harm behaviour. In 1993, an American professor in psychology, Marsha Linehan, found that most self-harmers exhibit mood-dependent behaviour, that is, they tend to act in accordance with their current feelings rather than consider long-term desires and goals.

Two years later, the psychiatrist S. Herpetz found some common observations among people who self-harm. These include a/an:
- inability to control emotions (poor affect regulation),
- impulsivity and aggressiveness,
- great deal of suppressed anger and high levels of self-directed hostility,
- inability to prioritise and plan ahead for the immediate or distant future.

Other researchers noticed that self-harm acts tend to increase when there were increased levels of chronic anger and anxiety. Typically, individuals who hurt themselves tend to possess or exhibit certain personality attributes, psychological characteristics and stress-coping styles.

Personality attributes
- Hypersensitive to rejections and criticisms
- Chronically angry (usually at themselves)
- Impulsive (lack impulse control)
- Easily irritable
- High level of aggressive feelings, which they disapprove strongly and often suppress or direct inward

Psychological characteristics
- Strong dislike of themselves or tendency to invalidate themselves
- Tendency to act in accordance with their current mood
- Depressed and suicidal/self-destructive
- Suffer chronic anxiety
- Perceive themselves as unable to cope with stress
- Low self-esteem and pessimistic about life
- Diffident about being able to control life
- Sense of being powerless to change things

Stress coping styles
- Tendency to suppress anger
- Not plan for the future
- Avoidance of problems
- Being inflexible

In a 2013 study conducted in Changi General Hospital (Tay & Cheng, 2014), 37 adults who self-harmed were screened for maladaptive personality traits. The majority (89.2 per cent) screened positive for more than one class of maladaptive traits. The three most prevalent classes of maladaptive traits were anankastic (obsessive-compulsive), schizoid (asocial or socially aloof) and paranoid (suspicious and distrustful). More than three quarters of the participants had three or more classes of maladaptive traits. The study concluded that maladaptive personality traits are common and inherent in self-harm patients.

WHY DO PEOPLE
INTENTIONALLY HARM THEMSELVES?

PART 2

> 💬 People cope with their problems differently.
> When things get worse for me by the day,
> the only way for me to cope is to hurt myself. 💬
> — Angela

It can be difficult for family members, friends and teachers to understand why someone they love or know is self-harming. It can make these same people, who are supposed to be loving and caring toward self-harmers, feel angry and upset. Not being able to stop a loved one from hurting herself or seeing her bleeding or injured can be distressing.

2.1   WHY DO CHILDREN AND YOUNG PERSONS WANT TO HURT THEMSELVES?

People resort to self-harm as a means of coping with pain and difficulties. Some of these difficulties may include anxiety, depression, bullying, discrimination, social isolation, failure in school, being abused and family breakdown. Self-harm can also be the result of many other problems that people face in their everyday lives. People who intentionally hurt themselves often harbour strong feelings of:

- self-hatred,
- fear,
- worry,
- guilt,
- depression,
- embarrassment,
- loneliness.

There is often an immense sense of helplessness and of losing control. Self-harm soon becomes a way of dealing with emotional pain and distress and the pressures of modern living. Self-harm often fulfills more than one function, particularly if it was done regularly. To self-harmers, the act may be perceived as a form of "self-medication". Here are some common reasons why young people deliberately harm themselves.

Self-harm gives individuals a sense of control

People who self-harm may feel trapped and desperate about their problems and do not know how to get help.

> You can't control what's happening around you but you can control what you do to yourself.

Self-harm relieves negative emotions and tension

People who self-harm sometimes describe a feeling of immense relief from overwhelming feelings—like anger, frustration, anxiety, sadness and misery—and their accompanying pressures. Some see self-harm as a means of converting an unbearable emotional pain into a physical form which helps keep them from doing something worse, such as attempting suicide.

> It helped me make the [emotional] pain go away. The more I cut myself, the more I wanted to do it. It was effective for me.

Self-harm serves as a form of punishment

People who self-harm may feel guilty or ashamed over something they have done or an event that happened to them but which was out of their control. This guilt and shame could be very unbearable.

> I hate myself for letting them abuse me in my childhood. I think I deserve to get hurt and feel pain.

Self-harm gives a feeling of being more "connected" and "alive"

Some self-harmers feel numb and detached from the world they live in and harming themselves reminds them they are still very much alive. Self-harm serves as a way to cope with very traumatic experiences like physical or sexual abuse.

> Seeing blood coming out seems to bring a sense of calmness and warmth. It reminds me that I am alive.

Other reasons why people hurt themselves
- Communicate to others the extent of their internal emotional turmoil
- Gain attention from adults or peers
- Express or repress their sexuality
- Obtain a feeling of euphoria (a "rush" or "high"), just as one would get from a drug addiction
- Prevent something worse from happening, like suicide
- Obtain and maintain influence over the behaviour of others
- Continue the abusive patterns that happened in childhood
- Distract themselves from their emotional troubles with physical ones

2.2   MY FOUR-YEAR-OLD SON HITS HIMSELF WHEN HE IS ANGRY. IS THIS NORMAL AND DOES IT MEAN HE IS LIKELY TO RESORT TO SELF-HARM ACTS WHEN HE IS OLDER?

It can be normal for a young child to resort to hitting himself when angry or frustrated, especially when the child has difficulties expressing himself or articulating what he wants.

Typically, a child may feel upset or distressed by various situational factors such as hunger, in pain, being ignored by adults, having his favourite toy taken away from him or feeling uncomfortable after soiling himself. The child would normally express the displeasure and discomfort by crying. This serves to gain the attention of his caregiver who would console him and remedy the problem. A small minority may resort to physical means such as throwing a tantrum or hitting themselves to achieve a similar effect. If the child is consistently reassured of his parents' love for them and receives positive attention, this form of self-harm would usually stop over time. But if the reason behind the behaviour is to gain attention, then being overly anxious or overprotective towards the child may have the unwanted effect of perpetuating the behaviour.

What parents can do is to offer distractions to stop the behaviour or to apply the "holding method"—hold the child from behind as if you are hugging him from behind while holding both his wrists with your hands for a period of time, during which you request that he counts along with you to calm him down. Parents should then show or demonstrate to the child another healthier way to express his distress such as speaking to an adult caregiver. Thank or compliment the child for bringing his distress up to an adult and keeping himself safe. This strategy usually works. Parents need not worry too much about this behaviour in young children because they typically will learn more adaptive ways to express themselves as they grow up.

2.3   HOW DO VERY YOUNG CHILDREN AND THOSE WITH INTELLECTUAL DEFICIENCIES EXPRESS THEIR DISTRESS?

Very young children, due to their limited verbal skills and cognitive development, may not be able to process information in a mature manner or express their feelings and thoughts in a meaningful way that can be easily understood by adults. Feeling helpless that no one can understand or help them, they may hurt themselves out of frustration or anger. If self-harm helps a child to achieve what he wants, like gaining his parents' attention or having his parents give in to his demands, he may then utilise self-harm more frequently in future to meet his needs.

Self-harm could also happen in children with severe intellectual deficiencies. They might bite, hit or bang themselves on hard surfaces with little awareness of pain. Although these behaviours seem to be extreme, they serve self-soothing and sensation-seeking purposes.

It is important for parents, healthcare and teaching professionals to understand the cause(s) of distress, the mechanism and purpose of such actions so as to respond appropriately. Parents should seek professional help if the self-harming behaviour:

- persists despite parental intervention,
- is extremely dangerous and causes excessive injury, or potentially even death,
- is incomprehensible to adults, thereby making it difficult for them to intervene.

CASE STUDY

Amy was 16 years old when she first began to cut herself. Active in sports and school club activities, she appeared outgoing and carefree to her friends. Her parents described her as strong-headed and emotional.

She had a boyfriend of the same age and with a similar family background. Having been hurt in previous failed relationships, Amy was very possessive over him. She expected him to call her daily and was unable to accept that he had other more important things to attend to instead of being with her. Their relationship soured when she saw him speaking to another girl. Unable to accept what she saw, she went home and smashed a mirror in her bedroom. She then impulsively took a broken piece of glass and cut herself on her wrist.

Since that incident, Amy would feel increasingly agitated and emotional whenever she quarreled with her boyfriend. Once, she took a penknife and proceeded to cut her forearm with it. With each cut, she would feel a release of tension and, very quickly, a feeling of numbness would creep all over her. The cutting seemed to take on a life of its own.

Thereafter, she would use cutting to vent her frustration and to express her anger and disappointment.

Initially cutting herself over relationship problems, she began to cut for other reasons such as an unsatisfactory exam result and even normal day-to-day stressors. Her boyfriend was unable to persuade her to stop cutting herself and soon left her, believing that Amy had begun to use self-harm to manipulate and control him.

COMMON MISCONCEPTIONS ABOUT PEOPLE WHO SELF-HARM

PART 3

People often fear what they do not understand and this can include any behaviour that does not conform to society's norms. Invariably, they discriminate, avoid and even look down on individuals who self-harm without actually knowing the reasons behind the behaviour.

Only when we are informed and more educated about the issues of self-harm are we then able to understand and empathise with the sufferers of self-harm. Self-harmers need us to help them stop the very behaviour that torments them.

MYTH 1: PEOPLE WHO HARM THEMSELVES ARE OUT TO SEEK ATTENTION

Many people, and these include family members, friends, teachers and even health professionals, often view self-harmers as attention-seeking.

Unfortunately, it is foolish to dismiss any act of deliberate self-harm as a ploy to seek attention. In fact, most people who harm themselves feel strongly that they are not trying to seek attention. For some, the privacy and secrecy of the act itself gives them a sense of control which they find beneficial. Even if there is an element of attention-seeking, we should take such acts seriously and explore the feelings of the person who hurt himself.

MYTH 2: PEOPLE WHO HARM THEMSELVES ARE A DANGER TO OTHERS

People who harm themselves do so as a means of releasing negative emotions like anger and frustration. Most will not hurt other people because they care about others more than they care about themselves.

Interviews and surveys with self-harming individuals have revealed that they had no desire to take aggression out on others. For them, self-harming was a way of releasing pent-up anger without having to fight or argue with someone else.

MYTH 3: SELF-HARMERS ARE EMOTIONALLY WEAK

Many people perceive individuals who harm themselves as being emotionally weak and might even look down on them. This perception is wrong and foolish.

People who self-harm do not simply hurt themselves because they like it or really want to. They have probably struggled with their problems internally for a very long time, undergoing tremendous emotional stress and pain at the same time. As self-harm provides an immediate relief of distress, it readily becomes a very convenient outlet—even normal people may occasionally slam doors and smash things to vent their frustrations and anger.

In this light, self-harmers are seen as having an alternative but nonetheless maladaptive way of coping with their stress. Gradually, self-harmers may "learn" to adopt self-harm as an "effective" means of relieving tension.

MYTH 4: PEOPLE WHO SELF-HARM CRAVE PAIN

Most young persons who injure themselves do not possess a craving for physical pain. Neither do they enjoy nor derive pleasure from the pain the way masochists or sadists do.

As self-harmers persist in their injuring acts, they often feel Increasingly numb towards the pain and are gradually able to increase their tolerance to the pain. As such, the injury may become more serious over time.

Very rarely do self-harmers actually enjoy inflicting physical pain on themselves. It is the process of diverting away or substituting the emotional pain with physical pain that is beneficial to them.

THE CAUSES OF
SELF-HARM BEHAVIOURS

PART 4

Studies conducted at Coventry University, UK, and case studies from the NCH, a children's charity organisation in the UK, revealed that the onset of self-harm is often linked to difficulties in the young person's life. These difficulties include factors such as:

- being bullied at school,
- parental divorce,
- death of a loved one,
- an unwanted pregnancy.

The findings also suggested that self-harm was a significant but often hidden problem. More was needed to help those who deliberately hurt themselves.

Most of the time, it is the interplay of several factors that contribute towards self-harm. These factors include past traumatic experiences, negative mindsets and abnormalities in brain physiology and chemistry.

4.1   TO WHAT EXTENT DO PAST TRAUMATIC EXPERIENCES LEAD TO SELF-HARM?

The risk of self-harm increases when children have been physically or sexually abused, physically or emotionally neglected or when subjected to chaotic family conditions brought upon by marital discord between parents. Individuals who do not have a sense of being loved are likely to be least able to control their destructive impulses.

Children invariably suffer low self-esteem if they grow up in an environment where their feelings are not validated or acknowledged, and where they are frequently put down by caregivers. The children eventually do not develop three important self-capacities, namely:

- an ability to maintain a sense of self-worth,
- an ability to tolerate strong emotions,
- an ability to maintain a sense of connection to others.

These children can never feel they are good enough when their existence and accomplishments are met with hostile silence, harsh words or abusive actions. They cannot also develop fully the ability to tolerate and integrate strong emotions when such feelings are met with punishment or derision. So they begin to perceive themselves to have less control over problem-solving options and as time goes by, avoid problems as a means of coping. This feeling of disempowerment may in turn be related to the long periods of being rejected by their parents who disregarded their feelings and opinions as they were growing up.

4.2   IS SELF-HARM CAUSED BY ABNORMALITIES IN BRAIN PHYSIOLOGY AND CHEMISTRY?

Brain physiology and chemistry may play a role in determining who deliberately sets out to harm himself and who does not. A study found that people who self-harm tend to be extremely angry, impulsive, anxious and aggressive. Interestingly, it also revealed that these self-harmers had lower levels of serotonin, a major chemical neurotransmitter, in the brain. Serotonin acts on specific receptors located at the limbic system which is the epicentre or cradle for emotions and aggressive feelings. The study thus presented evidence that some of the characteristics of anger, impulsiveness, anxiety and aggression may be linked to a deficit of serotonin in the brain. Other studies seem to suggest that irritable people with relatively normal serotonin function express their irritation outwardly, while people with low serotonin function turn the irritability inward by self-damaging or committing suicidal acts. This suggests that the reason for self-harming behaviour may well be biological, and one that is possibly influenced by genetics as well.

4.3   DO CERTAIN MINDSETS CONTRIBUTE TOWARDS SELF-HARM BEHAVIOUR?

In the cognitive model of treatment approach, it is believed that a person's thinking and feelings are closely linked together and due to the nature of this link, they affect each other. So when a person has positive and realistic thoughts, he is likely to feel better and behave in a more productive way. A person with pessimistic and negative thoughts would feel worse off and behave in a less adaptive manner. Some other common thinking errors include:

- jumping to conclusions: making haste conclusions without determining all the facts,
- all-or-none thinking (black-and-white thinking): thinking that it has to be "this way and no other way" or only able to consider either opposing extremes during a situation or event,
- tunnel vision: being only able to see one singular outcome which is often unrealistic or overly negative,

- catastrophising: inaccurate amplification of an otherwise small situation to a huge problem or crisis.

A person with these thinking errors interprets events unrealistically and in a disproportionate magnitude. What is originally a trivial event gets blown out of proportion and appears disastrous to the person. He may also subconsciously ignore the positive and good aspects of things or may be too quick to conclude that whatever has happened is bad for him.

Attribution Bias
Attribution bias describes a certain negative mindset where the person:
- readily assumes personal blame for negative events,
- expects that one negative experience is part of a pattern of many other negative events to follow,
- believes that a currently negative situation will continue permanently.

There are suggestions that a relationship exists between attribution bias and self-harm. The person reacts passively, helplessly and ineffectively to negative events. He may feel that things will never go right no matter what he does. He may then reject other people's help, withdraw himself from others, react emotionally to negative events or avoid similar experiences in future. Such pessimism prevails even with positive events.

Individuals who self-harm may experience these same thinking errors and appraise events as totally negative and catastrophic.

4.4   DOES DEPRESSION LEAD TO SELF-HARM?
Some individuals who self-harm are found to be dysphoric. They experience a depressed mood with a high degree of irritability, sensitivity to rejection and underlying tension.

There is usually some interpersonal stressor that increases the level of dysphoria and tension to an unbearable degree. This feeling persists even when the person is not actively hurting himself. When he hurts himself, though, he achieves a quick and effective release of physiological tension and arousal.

Self-harm consequently becomes a preferred coping mechanism as it acts to reduce both physiological and emotional stress dramatically and quickly.

Due to this mechanism of behaviour conditioning, the sensory stimulation that is associated with self-harm may operate as a negative reinforcer and further maintain and prolong the self-harm behaviour.

4.5   CAN ONE LEARN SELF-HARM FROM OTHERS OR FROM THE ENVIRONMENT—THE CONTAGION EFFECT?

Self-harm can, to a certain extent, be "learnt", especially after a young person watches or hears about a close friend doing it. He may become curious and wish to experiment. Fortunately, this is rare and it would be under very extraordinary circumstances for a young person to emulate another person in this way. For emotionally-stable teens with good social and family support, the risk of copying self-harming behaviour is considerably lower.

There are some concerns that self-harm acts may also be imitated by the young through newspaper reports, television, the Internet and new social media. This contagion effect could occur with intensive reporting of, say, a celebrity or famous person who engaged in such an act. It is also relatively easy for teens to access self-harm stories, images and videos online. Even fictional and romanticised representations of a self-harm behaviour in a popular movie or television programme can assert some influence on the young mind. However, there is still controversy as to the relationship between media representations of self-harm and actual self-harm behaviour.

Another concern is the education of school-going teenagers on self-harm issues. For example, some school-based youth self-harm and suicide prevention programmes could have the unintended effect of suggesting that self-harm and suicide are options for many young people. However, this definitely is not the intended message.

Similarly, widespread distribution of lists of self-harm and suicide warning signs, which may highlight common behaviours among distressed persons that are not specific for self-harm and suicide, can promote such acts as possible solutions to ordinary distress. Inaccurate portrayal of facts and improper conveyance of health messages may even suggest that suicidal thoughts and behaviours are normal responses to stress.

As these examples indicate, any prevention efforts must be carefully planned, implemented and evaluated.

4.6   IS IT TRUE THAT INDIVIDUALS WHO SELF-HARM CANNOT EXPRESS THEMSELVES EMOTIONALLY?

A group of researchers positively linked alexithymia to self-injurious behaviour. Alexithymia describes the inability for an individual recognise and describe one's emotions, defining them instead in terms of physical somatic sensations or behavioural reactions. Rather than using words to express feelings, the individual may utilise self-harm as one of the means to communicate to others the extent of his emotional turmoil and pain. It is important to note that alexithymia per se does not typically lead to acts of self-harm.

4.7   TO WHAT EXTENT DO PSYCHIATRIC CONDITIONS CONTRIBUTE TOWARDS SELF-HARMING BEHAVIOURS?

Young persons who engage in self-harm behaviours may be suffering from acute or chronic psychiatric conditions. These include:

- Borderline Personality Disorder,
- Depression,
- Post-traumatic Stress Disorder,
- Dissociative Disorders,
- Eating Disorders,
- Anxiety Disorders (includes Panic Disorder and Obsessive Compulsive Disorder),
- Bipolar Mood Disorder,
- Impulse-control Disorder.

In a local study (Loh, Teo & Lim, 2013) surveying new psychiatric outpatients in a general hospital between 2006 and 2010, 23.6 per cent of 542 new patients aged between 12 to 19 years reported self-harm. Self-harm was positively associated with mood disorders, adjustment disorders and regular alcohol use. However, there was no association with parental marital status, anxiety disorder, habitual smoking or family history of psychiatric illness. Children are not excluded from these disorders even though the rates of these conditions occurring are substantially lower. In times of acute emotional stress, children may react negatively and impulsively and go on to hurt themselves. These psychological conditions are explained in greater detail in Part 5 of this book.

Note that self-harm seen in Autistic Spectrum Disorders (autism) and Factitious Disorders (disorders characterised by deliberate production of physical or psychological symptoms in order to assume a sick role) are not discussed in this book as they tend to arise from underlying mechanisms such as neuro-developmental, personality and other psychological causes.

ASSOCIATED DISORDERS OF
SELF-HARM BEHAVIOURS

PART 5

More often than not, young persons who self-harm also suffer from other underlying psychological conditions. These associated conditions could arise:
- in vulnerable individuals, such as those with a strong family history of psychiatric illnesses,
- as part of the individual's own genetic makeup,
- because of stressful or traumatic life events,
- because of dysfunctional family backgrounds.

Ultimately, these psychological conditions significantly increase the risk of self-harming behaviours. It is thus important to understand what they are.

5.1   BORDERLINE PERSONALITY DISORDER

Borderline Personality Disorder is a common association with self-harm. It is characterised by:
- poor tolerance to stress,
- poor ability to monitor and regulate one's moods,
- self-identity disturbance,
- frustration,
- impulsive streaks.

Individuals with this disorder cope with stress differently and tend to use extreme or risky measures, such as self-harm, to cope with what they perceive to be rejection by others. (Borderline Personality Disorder is discussed on page 32.) There are three identifiable symptoms for this disorder.
- Volatility factor: This is characterised by inappropriate anger, unstable relationships and impulsive behaviour.
- Self-destructive/Unpredictable factor: This is characterised by self-harm behaviours and emotional instability.
- Identity Disturbance factor: This is self-identity crisis or the conflict between what a person really is, thinks he is and what others expect him to be.

5.2   DEPRESSION

Depression is a serious condition that can strike up to 5 per cent of children between nine and 17 years of age. According to population studies, the occurrence rate in a year increases from 0.4 per cent in children to as high as 8.3 per cent in adolescents. Individuals with this disorder fall into a prolonged period of depressed mood where they:

- lose interest in activities that they once enjoyed,
- are unable to sleep,
- lose their appetite,
- perpetually feel tired,
- are indecisive,
- have problems concentrating in studies or tasks,
- may neglect their personal appearance and hygiene.

They also tend to adopt negative thinking such as they believe they are not being loved by others. Consequently, they feel helpless and hopeless. Some depressed children and adolescents also become irritable, which may lead to aggressive behaviour. Depressed adolescents with self-harm tend to be younger, perceive less support from the family and use more alcohol. Depressed teens are also at higher risk for suicidal behaviour in addition to self-harm (Tuisku et al, 2009).

5.3   POST-TRAUMATIC STRESS DISORDER

Post-Traumatic Stress Disorder (PTSD) refers to the conglomeration of anxiety symptoms that a person experiences after a threatening or traumatic event. The earlier theory that the event must be life-threatening is no longer valid because each person's reaction to, and interpretation of, a traumatic experience is personal and unique.

The harm that PTSD sufferers inflict on themselves could be seen as an attempt to control seemingly uncontrollable and frightening emotions associated with the trauma. In psychodynamic terms, women who are traumatised suffer a sort of internal "split" of consciousness. When the women go into a self-harming episode, their conscious and subconscious minds take on roles of the abuser (the one that harms), the victim and the non-protecting bystander. Younger groups of children who would have difficulty understanding and interpreting their life experiences, especially the traumatic ones, may constantly re-enact the hurt through self-harm acts such as biting, knocking themselves and other destructive behaviours. This is their attempt to gain control and mastery over the distressing experiences and associated feelings.

5.4   EATING DISORDERS

Self-harm behaviour is often seen in females with anorexia and bulimia. Up to 5 per cent of females with eating disorders had previously self-harmed.

Anorexia Nervosa

This is a disease in which a person is obsessed with losing weight. The person adopts a strict diet or fasts, exercises excessively and possesses a distorted body image. The person also evaluates herself negatively based on her weight. To an extreme, it can cause serious medical conditions such as anaemia, electrolyte imbalance and heart failure.

Bulimia Nervosa

This is an eating disorder marked by food binging at discrete periods of time followed by purging, whereby the person attempts to remove the food from her body. Common methods for purging are self-induced vomiting and overusing laxatives. As with anorexia, dangerous medical complications can arise.

Studies on women with these eating disorders show that self-harm acts bring about a rapid release from tension and anxiety, and this probably serves as a motivation for an eating disordered person to hurt herself. Self-harm may also serve as an alternative to fasting or purging.

5.5   ANXIETY DISORDERS

Anxiety disorders, which include Obsessive Compulsive Disorder (OCD) and Panic Disorder, can cause great distress. Individuals with anxiety disorders may sometimes use self-harm as a self-soothing, coping mechanism as it brings about fast and temporary relief from the tension that builds up as they become progressively more anxious.

Obsessive Compulsive Disorder (OCD)

People with OCD typically exhibit excessive and repetitive hand-washing, checking, number counting, reassurance seeking and other ritualistic behaviours despite knowing that the acts are silly and senseless. For some, they may feel compelled to perform self-harm acts which could include peeling and cutting their skin, pulling of hair or picking on fresh wounds. Thankfully, self-harm behaviours are usually not common in OCD.

The intrusiveness of self-harm thoughts and compulsions cause great distress. By hurting themselves, individuals obtain relief from anxiety and distress. Many are aware of the senselessness of their behaviour but are unable to disengage from the compulsive behaviour.

People suffering from anxiety disorders often believe that by carrying out the physical or mental ritual, they would be able to prevent something bad from happening. This "magical thinking" is a characteristic feature of OCD. Current scientific studies have pointed the cause of OCD to an imbalance in the neuro-transmitter serotonin in the brain. Medical treatment for OCD is therefore important.

Panic Disorder

Sufferers of Panic Disorder wrongly interpret their bodily symptoms as catastrophic and imminent of a dangerous outcome. For example, a sufferer might believe that the pain he is feeling in his belly is the beginning of a heart attack. The distress that sufferers feel is so overwhelming that they may resort to self-harm acts to calm their feelings. They fail to realise that the physical symptoms are part of a normal bodily reaction to stress.

5.6 IMPULSE CONTROL DISORDER

Individuals with this disorder are unable to resist an impulse or urge to perform acts that are potentially harmful to themselves or others.

With regard to self-harm, there is a sense of increasing tension or arousal before committing the self-harm act and this is followed by pleasure, gratification or release of tension at the time of the act. The person is consciously aware of his act and there might be self-reproach or guilt feelings after the self-harm has taken place. This cycle of mounting tension-release-regret is typically described and experienced by many self-harmers.

5.7 DISSOCIATIVE DISORDERS

Dissociative Disorders involve problems of consciousness. Individuals could experience either amnesia, fragmented consciousness or an alteration of consciousness. In fact, normal people dissociate too. For example, when driving on a long and uninteresting expressway, you may find that your mind is not actually concentrating on the driving but you are still able to manoeuvre the vehicle safely and quickly return to self-awareness to avert danger if the need arises.

In this disorder, the individual feels detached from his own body and there is a sense of numbness and not being in control. To counteract that sensation and to stop the unreal feelings, the person inflicts physical injury on himself, hoping that the pain will bring him back to self-awareness. Although dissociation is more common in adults, it could also occur in younger children and teenagers.

5.8   BIPOLAR MOOD DISORDER

This unique mood disorder is characterised by one or more episodes of mania (abnormal and persistent elevation in mood state) alternating with subsequent episodes of depression. Typically, a person with mania would exhibit:

- grandiose ideas,
- an inflated self-esteem,
- increased impulsivity and physical activity,
- a decreased need for sleep,
- willingness to participate in reckless or potentially dangerous behaviours.

People with a Bipolar Mood Disorder may have psychotic symptoms such as delusions (false beliefs that are usually of the grandiose type) and hallucinations (usually hearing voices or seeing things that are not there). In a manic state, the person may end up hurting himself, particularly when he is emotionally agitated, deluded and impulsive. When the mood swings to that of depression, the person may experience a similar degree of hopelessness and helplessness as one would in a major depressive illness. In such a case, self-harm could be an option for him to ameliorate his mood symptoms.

5.9   PSYCHOTIC DISORDER

An individual who suffers from psychotic disorders such as schizophrenia typically experience distorted realities, hallucinations and delusions. He might react to his hallucinations commanding him to harm himself or he may be deluded that there is something wrong within his body resulting in his trying to get rid of that something through self-cutting. Again, the underlying mechanisms here are very different from the larger group of non-psychotic people who self-harm. Such individuals would invariably require psychotropic medications in a psychiatric care facility for safety reasons.

SELF-HARM AND TEEN SUICIDE

When one talks about deliberate self-harm, it is inevitable that the topic of teen suicide is raised for discussion. Both share similar characteristics of being self-inflicted and frequently co-exist in an individual. Both are destructive in nature. By choosing self-harm or suicide as a means of escaping from pain or inflicting guilt on another person, the individual is undergoing a lot of emotional and psychological disturbance.

Despite several similarities between suicide and self-harm, the motivation and intent behind them are different:

- Young persons who self-harm do not actually intend to die. Instead, they want to release the tensions they feel and use self-harm as an outlet for their pent-up feelings.
- Those who plan and go on to attempt suicide genuinely wish to die and may proceed to complete the suicide. They invariably feel hopeless and see no way out of the predicament they are in.

While both self-harm behaviours and suicidal tendencies could co-exist in the same person, they also occur in isolation. Some survivors of suicide attempts have said that they actually started off harming themselves first for a long period of time before progressing to attempting suicide. Hence, there is an overlap of individuals who engage in self-harm acts and those who attempt suicide.

6.1   WHAT IS SUICIDE?

Suicide is the act of killing oneself deliberately. It is a very personal act and one that is deliberately chosen as a way of solving problems. A person commits suicide when his world becomes intolerable, meaningless and hopeless. In fact, a sense of hopelessness is one of the key factors in predicting suicide in all age groups. The motivation to commit suicide could be multiple—to escape from hurt, suffering or shame, or even as a form of revenge.

Of all suicides, those involving young persons evoke the greatest shock, horror and disbelief. The loss of a young child or teenager is unnecessary, senseless and wasteful. It is not just a loss to his family and friends, but also a loss to society.

6.2   HOW COMMON IS SUICIDE AMONG CHILDREN AND TEENAGERS IN SINGAPORE?

In any society, suicide in children below 12 years of age is very rare, and this is also true for Singapore where the population is small. In 2012, there were 17 cases of completed suicides in the 10–19 years age group as compared to 10 in 2006. Though the suicide rate for children and adolescents remains among the lowest in the world at between one or two per 100,000 young persons, there is still some concern of an increasing trend in suicidal behaviour locally.

6.3   HOW IMPORTANT IS A HISTORY OF ATTEMPTED SUICIDE IN COMPLETING AN ACT OF SUICIDE?

A history of attempted suicide is the single most important risk factor of suicide. In Western countries, some 25 per cent to 50 per cent of young persons who completed suicide previously tried to kill themselves.

In 1978, practising psychiatrist B H Chia found that 15 per cent of young persons who committed suicide in Singapore had a past history of attempted suicide. In his follow-up study of 158 young suicide attempters, 7 per cent eventually committed suicide. In yet another five-year study, those who attempted suicide several times were found to have a higher risk of completed suicide than those who attempted suicide for the first time.

Another recent local study on attempted suicide in Chinese adolescents over the period 1991 to 1998 also revealed a rising trend in suicide attempts. The study also revealed that the numbers peaked in the month of October, just before school examinations are held. In children below 15 years old, attempted suicide is four to five times more common in girls.

Despite a suggested relationship between self-harm and suicide, there is no current local data on the number of teens who committed or attempted suicide and who were themselves, at one time or other, self-harmers.

6.4   WHY IS SUICIDE MORE WIDELY REPORTED THAN SELF-HARM?

Firstly, all cases of suicide have to be reported to the police and these cases are also scrutinised by the coroner. Also, it is harder to capture data on self-harm since scars can be hidden and overdosing on drugs is done privately. Many self-harmers also do not seek medical help or inform anyone about what they are doing. They may also not suffer severe medical complications that warrant medical attention. Hence, self-harm goes unreported and what we see is just the tip of the iceberg.

6.5   WHEN DO CHILDREN BEGIN TO THINK ABOUT SUICIDE?

Cognitively, the very young are deemed unable to understand the concept of death.

In 1999, psychologist Brian Mishara of the University of Quebec in Canada suggested that children already have an elaborate understanding of suicide and death by the time they are nine years old. However, this theory remains controversial as some experts feel that such an understanding can only arise after early adolescence when the child begins to have an awareness of self and a concept of death. Before that, most children would see themselves as omnipotent due to their egocentricity. Younger children are also less likely to attempt suicide because they do not have the cognitive ability to plan and carry out such acts.

In the context of self-harm, when a teenager harms himself repeatedly despite intervention, there is a higher risk of subsequent suicide attempt. However, research also suggests that the increase in suicide rates with age may be due to increased exposure to critical risk factors such as severe depression, drugs and alcohol. Studies have found that for younger children exposed to these risk factors, the suicide rate is similar to that for older teens.

6.6   WHAT ARE THE RISK FACTORS THAT PARENTS SHOULD LOOK OUT FOR?

Suicide is a complex behaviour that is usually caused by a combination of factors in the absence of protective factors. Researchers have identified a number of risk factors associated with a higher risk for suicide. In his book on young suicides, B H Chia found that in Singapore:
- predisposing risk factors are mental illness, personality disorder and chronic substance abuse,
- precipitating risk factors are job and financial problems, relationship problems and social problems.

Mental illness

Generally, individuals with diagnosed mental illness and disorders are at an increased risk for suicide. The majority who attempt suicide have either some form of psychosis such as schizophrenia, major depression or severe anxiety disorder.

Personality disorder

Overseas studies suggest similar personality characteristics among the young who committed suicide. The most common characteristics observed were "withdrawn, lonely, super-sensitive and angry". Top on the list of personality disturbance in the young suicides were those:

- with borderline personalities (emotion regulation difficulties, identity problems and impulsivity),
- who were antisocial (recklessness, little regard for others and authority).

Chronic substance abuse

Although not a major problem among the young in Singapore, drugs and alcohol do impair one's judgment and increase one's impulsivity level. Long-term use can also suppress mood, leading to depression. Together with unemployment, relationship breakdowns and other psychosocial stresses, many develop secondary depression as well. In adult groups, alcoholism is associated with up to a 15 per cent risk of completed suicide.

Relationship problems

Young persons who commit suicide tend to come from families where there were neglect, abuse and assault. Long-term interpersonal problems with parents or siblings and severe relationship breakdown with members of the opposite sex can precipitate acute stress reactions, depressive thoughts and subsequent suicide ideations.

Job and financial problems

Job and financial problems are less prevalent as most young persons would still be in school. However, financial problems may force some teens to leave school prematurely to start working. Faced with limited life skills and working experience, they frequently face challenges and may become depressed as a result. Many of those who attempted suicide expressed regret over the loss of educational opportunities.

Social problems

Enlistment into National Service and poor academic performance are less common precipitating causes for young suicide.

Newly-enlisted young males may develop adjustment reactions to the new and more regimental environment. Those who cannot tolerate the stress may act impulsively. Most do not want to die and their suicide attempts are generally a genuine cry for help.

Young persons who do badly or not good enough in examinations may feel depressed and frightened to face their parents. They feel that their parents will only love and approve of them if they excel in school. Notwithstanding that academic pressures are great in Singapore children, there is no evidence to suggest that suicide rate increases during examination periods or after students receive their school results.

6.7 ARE THERE ANY PROTECTIVE FACTORS AGAINST SELF-HARM AND TEEN SUICIDE?

Researchers have identified the protective factors that may reduce the likelihood of self-harm and suicidal behaviour. These can include an individual's genetic or neurobiological make-up, attitudinal and behavioural characteristics, and environmental attributes. Some identified protective factors are:

- Skills in problem-solving, impulse control, conflict resolution and non-violent handling of disputes.
- Strong family and community support.
- Easy access to effective and appropriate mental health care and support.
- Restricted access to highly lethal methods of suicide.
- Cultural and religious beliefs that discourage suicide and support self-preservation instincts.

Measures that enhance resilience are as essential as those that reduce the risks in preventing self-harm and suicide. Positive resistance to suicide is not permanent, so programmes that support and maintain protection against suicide should be ongoing.

6.8 TO WHAT EXTENT DOES GENDER INFLUENCE TEEN SUICIDE?

Biologically, males are more active and tend to "act out" physically. Girls, on the other hand, tend to verbalise their feelings of frustration and sadness without the fear of being criticised because society allows them to do so. It has been postulated that for this reason, among several others, males commit suicide more than females. In the US, for instance, more than four times as many male youths die by suicide. Men are more likely to use more fatal and violent methods of suicide such as jumping off buildings, hanging or using firearms. These methods lead to a fatal outcome in 78 per cent to 90 per cent of the time.

In contrast, suicide attempts tend to be led by females who report higher rates of depression. Girls and women are more likely to ingest poisons, which are deemed as less lethal and more likely to give them a chance of rescue.

6.9   MY CHILD HAS A STRONG AND DIFFICULT PERSONALITY. SHOULD I BE WORRIED?

Although a young person's personality is not quite completely shaped in early adolescence, a trained psychiatrist or mental health professional might be able to detect some flaws or difficulties in his personality that could potentially cause unnecessary stress to themselves and their families. Hence the psychiatrist would be more inclined to use the term "personality traits" as opposed to attributing it as a disorder. Nevertheless, one should monitor the progression of the personality traits and seek professional help early if a clear pattern ensues.

One of the most challenging personality disorders to treat is manifested by Borderline Personality Disorder. Borderline Personality Disorder is widely seen in impulsive and risk-taking young individuals. People with this disorder might have multiple failed relationships or come from a chaotic and abusive family background. They tend to have problems with self-identity, regulating their emotions and maintaining stable relationships. This often leads to multiple break-ups and frustration. Being impulsive and intolerant of stress also increases the likelihood of self-harm behaviours and suicide risks.

6.10 WHAT KIND OF MENTAL ILLNESS PREDISPOSES A PERSON TO SUICIDE?

Research shows that over 90 per cent of young people who complete suicide have a diagnosable mental or substance abuse disorder or both, and that the majority have depressive illness. In a decade-long follow-up study of 73 overseas adolescents diagnosed with major depression, it was found that:
- seven per cent completed suicide some time later,
- depressed adolescents were five times more likely to have attempted suicide compared with a control group of age peers without depression,

- almost half of the teenagers who completed suicide had a previous contact with a mental health professional,
- aggressive, disruptive and impulsive behaviours are common attributes in youth of both sexes who complete suicide.

In Singapore, B H Chia found that among the young suicides, 23 per cent suffered from some form of mental illness, including depression, schizophrenia and mood disturbances. Many harboured strong negative feelings before they committed suicide. These feelings included anger, despair, grievance and hatred. In fact, when compared to older people who committed suicide, young suicides were more often associated with anger.

Schizophrenia and suicide

People with schizophrenia are likely to kill themselves if they cannot accept their condition. This is especially so if the disorder affects their relationship with loved ones and causes them to lose their jobs. Some commit suicide because they cannot tolerate the hallucinations and delusions or severe side effects to medications. Up to 15 per cent of patients with schizophrenia kill themselves eventually.

6.11 WHAT IS THE RISK OF YOUNG SUICIDE IF SOMEONE IN MY FAMILY HAS A MENTAL ILLNESS?

In both local and Western studies, it was found that the risk of young suicide increases if one or both parents are mentally ill.

In a study of youths who attended a private psychiatric clinic in Singapore, 16 per cent have family members who were mentally ill compared to 7.1 per cent in a control group without the positive family history. Four per cent have close relatives who had suicidal tendencies. In Western countries, this figure is greater at 25 per cent to 50 per cent.

However, we should note that the genetic disposition of suicide is independent of any genetic transmission of mental illness. As with self-harm, several studies have suggested that a low level of hydroxy-indoleacetic acid (5-HIAA), a metabolite of serotonin, in the spinal fluid leads to both attempted and completed suicides. The studies postulate that low levels of this neurotransmitter together with mental illness and overwhelming stressful life events might activate suicide triggers.

WARNING SIGNS OF SELF-HARM
BEHAVIOURS AND SUICIDE

PART 7

The symptoms of self-harm and suicidal tendencies vary from individual to individual. But they seldom occur without warning. While every self-harm act or suicide attempt is distinctly personal, a number of common signs are found. It is important for parents, teachers, friends and counsellors to look for these signs.

7.1   WHAT ARE THE WARNING SIGNS?

The warning signs can be categorised into five major groups:

Physical
- disturbed sleep pattern
- insomnia or hypersomnia (sleeping too much)
- deterioration in personal hygiene and grooming
- poor appetite
- binging on food
- chronic fatigue and lethargy
- unexpected scars and wounds

Social
- withdrawal from friends and family
- avoiding contact with people
- loss of interest in things and activities that were once enjoyed

Academic
- deterioration in school grades
- lack of motivation to study

Psychological
- frequent crying episodes
- depressed mood
- persistent anxiety
- irritable mood
- poor concentration
- excessive negative thinking
- talk of giving up
- sense of hopelessness

Conduct
- increased impulsivity
- increased defiance and opposition to authority figures
- increased minor offences and disciplinary problems
- use of alcohol and drugs

7.2   WHAT SHOULD I DO IF I SUSPECT MY CHILD IS FEELING DEPRESSED?

Find ways to talk with your child to find out how he feels. Teens often turn to friends their own age to share their thoughts and feelings as they feel too embarrassed to talk to their parents, teachers and elders. Be alert about stressful events such as a breakup in a relationship, a recent death of a significant person and failures in school. Take extra safety precautions by not having loose medicine lying around at home and keeping away sharp items from direct access.

7.3   WHAT ARE THE CLUES THAT PARENTS SHOULD LOOK OUT FOR?

People who harm themselves often refuse to wear clothes with short sleeves or take off their clothes during sports or at the pool. You should be concerned if your child suddenly does not want to expose his arms or legs when previously doing so was not an issue. Some may wear accessories like wrist bands to hide the scars on their arms. Take note of your child's behaviour and mood changes. Are they more irritable, moody or withdrawn than usual? Some teens would skip meals or hide in their bedrooms all day to avoid being questioned about what had happened to them. Look out for academic deterioration, difficulty with sleep, appetite changes and reluctance or refusal to meet people.

7.4   WHAT ARE THE WARNING SIGNS OF AN IMPENDING SUICIDE?

Feeling depressed

Some common signs of depression are anger, unhappiness, crying spells, mood swings, irritable mood, poor appetite, poor sleep, loss of interest in daily activities and hobbies, feeling tired all the time, poor concentration and poor memory recall.

The child might also withdraw socially from friends and suffer a drop in his grades in school. There can also be the occasional vague complaints about physical discomfort such as headaches and stomach aches.

Sense of helplessness and hopelessness

The child might talk about death, suicide and offer comments such as "I feel like giving up" or "Life has no meaning". Always consider such threats and comments very seriously. This sense of hopelessness is compounded by difficulties in communicating with parents, teachers and peers as well as perpetual difficulty in coping with stress.

Performing final acts

These include giving away valued personal items and possessions, bidding farewells to family and friends for no apparent reason, and writing suicide letters or text messages.

Reckless behaviours

People who are contemplating suicide may get involved in risky behaviours such as dangerous and drunk driving, drug taking and picking fights. They may be sexually promiscuous or run away from home. These behaviours could be messages to reflect their deep-seated agony and their inability to solve their problems. Younger children may not engage in reckless behaviours but what one might notice is an increase in conduct behavioural problems such as defiance and opposition toward parents and teachers.

Substance abuse

The young person may also start taking alcohol or drugs. He may become entrenched in a pattern of abuse which reduces his ability to estimate danger, lowers his guard, impairs his judgment and increases impulsive and other risky behaviours. Alcohol and drugs can themselves lead to depression and a sense of worthlessness.

Presence of abnormal behaviour

Strange and bizarre behaviour, mood and speech could indicate presence of a psychotic illness. Refer to the medical professionals immediately if there are examples of:

- talking or laughing to oneself,
- having abnormal and unwarranted suspicions,
- increased mood and behaviour agitation,
- displaying a threatening and aggressive behaviour including verbalisations of threats to harm oneself or others.

HOW PARENTS AND
TEACHERS CAN HELP

PART 8

Self-harm needs to be taken seriously because the effects can be dangerous and life-threatening. Apart from recognising the warning signs of self-harm behaviours, it is also important to respond to acts of self-harm in a calm and helpful manner. Sometimes people who self-harm are accused of seeking attention. They might also be seen as a threat to others. This is not usually the case and such misconceptions can lead to unhelpful attitudes and responses from other people. Above all, most people who set out to harm themselves need understanding and empathy.

8.1   PROVIDE UNDERSTANDING AND EMPATHY

It is important to listen to your teenager's worries and understand why he tried to harm himself. Acknowledge and accept that he is going through genuine pain. Stay calm and be constructive, no matter how upset you are. There is no point in making the situation worse by being angry.

Do not place judgment or regard self-harm as an act of manipulation intended to make you feel bad or guilty. Do not accuse your teenager of seeking attention. Even if you feel that was the reason, it probably was not intended as one. Set aside your personal feelings of fear about the self-harm behaviour and focus on what is going on with him. Finally, ask him how he wants you to help.

If you are a teacher, it is important to encourage your students to let you know if any of their classmates is in trouble, upset or shows signs of harming himself. Because friends often worry about betraying a confidence, you may need to impress on them that self-harm can be dangerous to life and should, therefore, not be kept a secret and that it is better to get help than suffer in silence.

8.2   SHOW YOUR SUPPORT BY NOT AVOIDING THE ISSUE OF SELF-HARM OR SUICIDE

Make the initial approach to talk about the issue. Talking factually about self-harming acts or even suicide does not encourage people to attempt them. By raising and discussing the issue, you open up channels of communication and encourage your teenager to begin to share his thoughts and feelings. Teens feel a sense of relief that they are able to talk about the frightening thoughts and feelings they have about suicide and death, and that another person understood them.

However, do not pressure your child if he is reluctant to share his feelings. Make it clear that he does not need to hurt himself to get love and care from you. Provide simple yet positive distractions like going for a movie or walking in the park. Let him know that you are not ignoring his feelings but instead, he can feel lousy and still do something nice.

8.3   BE A GOOD LISTENER

Reflect on the feelings behind the words your teenager is saying. Summarise or paraphrase his statements so he knows you have understood him. Offer love, compassion and support. Showing anger, hurt, resentment and outrage is not helpful and sometimes will make the teenager feel guilty and unimportant.

Avoid statements like:

- "What you should do now is..." (reflects a lack of respect of the person's feelings)
- "Everything will be alright." or "It's not that bad." (trivialises the feelings)
- "Why must you do this to us?" (sounds accusatory and inflicts sense of guilt)
- "Cutting yourself is wrong no matter what!" (sounds judgemental and indicates you are unaware of the deeper problems and feelings)

Helpful statements are:

- "You must have felt terrible and disappointed when you were not given the chance to explain yourself." (validates their feelings)
- "When you didn't pass your exams, you thought that there was no point in going on anymore." (paraphrasing their concerns makes them feel understood)

If you listen carefully, you can assess the seriousness of the teenager's self-harm act and see whether there was suicide intent behind it. If suicide was intended, ask him how he plans to end his life. The more detailed and thought-out the plan, the closer and more dangerous he is to committing suicide. If the date, method, venue and time have been planned, the risk would be much higher.

8.4   SHOW YOU WANT TO HELP EVEN IF YOU DO NOT KNOW ALL THE ANSWERS

Parents must continually stress that they love their teenager and that they want to help but they do not have all the answers. It is useful to acknowledge that while you are not experiencing your teenager's feelings, you want to understand and assist. You can say:

- "You might be right in saying that we don't understand what you are going through, but we want to understand because you are the most important person to us."
- "We may not have all the answers now but we want you to know that you can trust us and count on our help."
- "It is hard for me to know you are doing this to yourself. No matter what, I love you anyway."

8.5   SET REASONABLE LIMITS AS TO WHAT YOUR CHILD CAN DO

It is not easy to ask someone to simply stop hurting themselves especially if they have done so for a long period of time and if the self-harm has been helping them consistently to cope with bad feelings. Sometimes a more practical approach is to accept that the self-harm behaviour will take some time before it reduces in frequency or stops completely.

If your child insists on carrying out the self-harm act, then set reasonable limits within which he can carry out the act. By setting reasonable limits, we can perhaps limit the extent of any damage. You can set the limits by asking him to determine where, when, how and what he intends to do. This way, you can be more vigilant towards his behaviour and render the necessary aid. Setting limits may eventually deter him from carrying out the act if he knows that others are keeping a lookout for him.

Punishments generally are unhelpful. They just perpetuate the cycle of self-hatred and unpleasantness that leads to self-harm.

If you cannot engage your child or he rejects your advances, back off for a few days or weeks. Do not push him. Sometimes he needs time to decide to trust someone. Tell him that you do not understand why he does it but you are willing to listen.

8.6   ENSURE SAFETY

If a self-harm act has been committed, first make sure the person is safe. Do not panic. If the injury is not serious, treat the injury yourself by doing first aid or simply by providing him with a plaster or bandage. If it is serious, seek immediate medical advice.

8.7   OFFER HELP

There are many ways of helping. Most people get through life problems on their own or with help from friends and family. Self-harm is no different.

Some people who self-harm will find it helpful to talk to someone else. This could be a friend or family member, a youth worker, a doctor or nurse, a social worker, a teacher or a counsellor. However, some people might have had bad experiences with health professionals before so you should ask them first how they wish to be helped.

You could also think about what triggers the self-harm urges and whether anything else can be used to replace the self-harm behaviour. For example, when stress builds up, consider what else the child can do to relieve it.

Think also about the potential dangers and how they can be reduced. For instance, if your teenager continues to cut himself, encourage him to do so in a safe place where medical help is accessible rather than in a private place where he may not be able to get help at all. These alternatives and more are described further in Part 9 on how the individual can help himself.

Remember that self-harm can be a way of coping, so stopping the self-harm behaviour is not always the best thing to aim for immediately. Providing safety and understanding are more important in the short term.

STOPPING THE SELF-HARM BEHAVIOURS

PART 9

Deciding when to stop harming one's self is a very personal decision. Many young persons have contemplated stopping on many occasions but get so cooped up with their problems that they continue to hurt themselves. Others are ambivalent about stopping because they are afraid that they would lose their only means of relieving anger and stress. You should not coerce your child into stopping the behaviour. The only person who can stop the self-harm is the sufferer himself.

9.1 GIVE YOUR TEENAGER A CHECKLIST OF THINGS TO ASK HIMSELF

Ask your teenager whether he wants to stop hurting himself. To help him ascertain whether he is ready, present those three points to him for consideration:
- "You might not be able to stop self-harm completely, but you can certainly exert more control by choosing when and how much you harm yourself."
- "You can set limits for your self-harm."
- "You can take responsibility for the self-harm."

You will know if your child has decided that he is ready to stop his self-harm behaviour. He would indicate so or ask to work through his issues with a trained counsellor or mental health worker.

American psychologist Tracy Alderman (1997) came up with a helpful manual and checklist of items for the individual to ask himself before he begins to walk away from self-harm. He may not be able to give a positive answer to every single item in the list but the more he can set himself to do those items, the easier and closer he is to stopping the self-harm behaviour. These have been adapted as follows:

Checklist of questions
- "Do I have a solid emotional support system of friends, family and/or professionals that I can turn to if I feel like hurting myself?"
- "Are there two other people in my life that I can call if I feel like hurting myself?"
- "Are there three different people whom I can talk with about my self-harm?"
- "Do I have at least 10 things I can do instead of hurting myself?"
- "Do I have a place I can go to so as not to hurt myself?"

Checklist of statements
- "I am confident that I can remove all the things that I am likely to use to hurt myself."
- "I have told at least two people that I am going to stop hurting myself."
- "I am willing to feel uncomfortable, scared and frustrated."
- "I feel confident that I can endure the thought of hurting myself."
- "I want to stop hurting myself."

By answering positively to the questions and affirming the statements, the teenager gains a sense of power and control over his actions which encourage a change in his stress-coping strategies. He can begin to work towards these goals to strengthen his willpower and motivation to stop the self-harm behaviour.

9.2   SELF-INJURY 12-STEP PROGRAMME

Some self-help groups such as Self-harm Anonymous have adapted the Alcohol Anonymous 12-step Recovery Programme for use to combat self-harm. While it does not necessarily describe self-harm as similar to drug or alcohol addiction, the similarity lies behind its shared principles of recovery in that self-harmers often could find hope again through the 12 steps. These steps helped self-harmers understand that although they could not stop on their own, help is available. They could depend on each other, and on a higher power.

As recovering individuals begin to work through the 12 steps, they soon discover that they are more empowered to overcome self-harm one day at a time and that they do not need to harm themselves if they did not wish to. When individuals come together to work through self-harm in the Twelve-step Programme, the group dynamics also allow for emotional, psychological and spiritual support among each and every group member, eventually rendering them feeling stronger and more in control.

The 12 Steps (adapted from Alcoholics Anonymous)
1. We admitted that we were powerless over self-harm, that our lives had become unmanageable.
2. Came to believe that a power greater than ourselves could restore us to sanity.

3. Made a decision to turn our will and our lives over to the care of our Higher Power as we understood It.
4. Made a searching and fearless moral inventory of ourselves.
5. Admitted to our Higher Power, to ourselves, and to another human being the exact nature of our wrongs.
6. Were entirely ready to have It remove all these defects of character.
7. Humbly asked It to remove our shortcomings.
8. Made a list of all persons we had harmed, and became willing to make amends to them all.
9. Made direct amends whenever possible, except when to do so would injure them or others.
10. Continued to take personal inventory, and when we were wrong, promptly admitted it.
11. Sought through prayer and meditation to improve our conscious contact with our Higher Power as we understood It, praying only for knowledge of Its will for us and the power to carry that out.
12. Having had a spiritual awakening as a result of these steps, we tried to carry this message to other self-harmers and to practice these principles in all our affairs.

9.3   OFFER SUBSTITUTES FOR SELF-HARM

There are alternative methods that can help your child release tension and cope with the numbness that comes along with stress. These are useful because the intense emotions that provoke self-harm are transient in that they come and go in waves. If your teenager can tolerate one emotion, he is likely to be able to tolerate another without hurting himself. It means he gets stronger as he goes along. Here are some strategies.

Play the 15-minute game

Get him to play a 15-minute game whereby he postpones a self-harm act for 15 minutes whenever he feels like hurting himself. When the time is up, encourage him to postpone the act for another 15 minutes. This carries on for as long as he can take it. He might be able to postpone self-harm and tire the intent out till the next day.

Create a personal emergency kit

Your child can create his own emergency kit filled with objects and tasks to do. Depending on his age and interests, the items could include drawing pencils, paper, puzzles, a music CD, photographs of friends, a list of telephone numbers, an inspirational book or letters that are special to him. He can take out this kit whenever he feels the need to hurt himself and distract himself with the items in it. You could change the items in the kit once a month so that he has something new to keep him occupied.

Allow acceptable reactions to feelings

Allow your child to act out his tensions or anxieties in safe and non-harming ways. One way of doing this is to match the emotion he is feeling with an activity that produces a similar reaction to a self-harm act.

For example, if your child wants to punish himself, you could get him to squeeze a handful of ice cubes until it melts or snap a rubber band worn on his wrist. It will hurt but it will not leave scars. He might feel foolish at first but at least there is less guilt, if there was any to start with. This strategy helps him get through an intense moment without getting hurt. It also demonstrates that he can cope with distress without permanently injuring his body.

Allow your child to refine the techniques and devise more creative ways and coping mechanisms. This way, the urge to self-harm lessens and loses its hold on his life. By empowering himself to break the cycle, he forces himself to try new coping mechanisms and gain a sense of mastery.

Note that your child may still want to cut himself despite using these methods. Think of alternatives and try something totally different. Individualise his coping methods and tailor them to suit his needs. The trick is not to give up. Sometimes he has to keep trying many times before he takes up a new method.

When your child is angry, frustrated and restless, get him to direct his feelings at an inanimate object or do an activity that releases tension

- Squash an empty drink can
- Slash a cardboard box or an old T-shirt
- Hit a pillow or use a pillow to hit a wall
- Tear up a newspaper

- Break sticks
- Play the piano or water the plants
- Go for a run
- Jump up and down until tired
- Strike a ball with a racket

When your child feels sad, depressed and unhappy, get him to do something soothing and slow
- Take a hot bath or soak in a bubble bath
- Curl up in bed and listen to soothing music
- Burn sweet-smelling incense or use aromatherapy
- Apply nice body lotion to soothe the skin
- Speak to or visit a friend
- Eat an ice cream or a favourite snack
- Write down his thoughts and feelings on paper

By expressing his thoughts and feelings on paper, the emotions your child feels become clearer and appear more containable. Teach your child to use "feeling" words instead of describing what he intends to do. For example, he can write "I feel sad and disappointed when..." instead of "He does not like me enough to give me a call, I am going to cut myself." The key is to identify his emotions, triggers and stressors so that he can learn how to better deal with them in future, or how to avoid or lessen them.

When your child craves for sensation or feels unreal and numb, get him to do something that creates a sharp sensation
- Squeeze some ice cubes hard
- Place fingers on frozen food
- Bite into a hot chilli or eat wasabi
- Rub liniment or vapour rub under the nostrils
- Snap skin with a rubber band
- Take a cold shower
- Slap a tabletop hard
- Stomp feet on the ground

When your child wants focus, get him to do a task that requires precision and concentration
- Play chess or a challenging computer game
- Research a topic on the Internet
- Do needlework, knitting or craft-work
- Choose an object in the room and study it meticulously, noting down its colour, size, shape, texture, prints on it, etc.

When your child wishes to see blood
- Allow him to use a red-ink pen to mark the areas on his body he wishes to cut. Then put ice cubes on those areas. The ice cubes produce a tingling sensation on the skin. To make it more real, add red colour dye to the water before freezing it.

9.4   WHAT CAN I DO IF MY CHILD STILL WANTS TO HURT HIMSELF?
If you are faced with this situation, you can:
- allow him to decide beforehand exactly what he will allow himself to do and how much is considered enough,
- get him to stick to the limits he has set,
- "allow" him to injure himself (you know it would take a long time before they reduce or stop self-harm) while keeping him as safe as possible.

Tell your child that when he hurts himself alone, he has to always try to keep the injury to a minimum and apply basic first aid. On your part, you should set realistic limits and know what to do in times of emergency and when to seek medical attention. Do the minimum required to ease your child's distress. If he can manage that much, at least he will be exerting some control over his self-harm. Remember that every time he meets the emotional and psyche pain head-on, it loses a little of its grip on him.

> ❝ I feel good at the end of the day to be empowered to overcome this monster [self-harm] with the help and understanding of the people who cared for me, without judgment and without condemnation. ❞
> — a self-harm survivor

WHAT KIND OF PROFESSIONAL SUPPORT CAN I GET?

PART 10

Online and community support groups for self-harm are more prevalent in western countries such as the United States, Canada, the Netherlands, United Kingdom, Australia and New Zealand. This is likely due to a more pro-active self-help culture and heightened awareness of self-harm in these populations.

In Asia, self-harm is unfortunately still as stigmatising as other mental health illnesses and hence it is more difficult to organise activities around it. Some Asian countries like Japan and Korea have suicide-prevention programs (e.g. Korea's Strategies to Prevent Suicide (STOPS) project), while others have programmes that promote positive outcomes and prevention of problem behaviours (e.g., substance abuse, delinquency, violence, and youth pregnancy). Hong Kong's Project P.A.T.H.S. is one such youth development programme that focuses on the prevention of at-risk behaviours which are often associated with self-harm and suicide in secondary school students.

In Singapore, if you need professional help, you can obtain a referral at any polyclinic or general-practitioner clinic to see a team of professionals at a child and adolescent psychiatric outpatient clinic, such as the Child Guidance Clinic. The National University Hospital System also has specialist outpatient clinics for children and young persons. If you are in school, your school counsellor can link you up to a community-based programme called REACH, which is described in greater detail later in this chapter. Typically, the healthcare team consists of child psychiatrists, clinical psychologists, medical social workers and specialist nurses. Other allied health professionals could include occupational therapists and case managers. Inpatient and outpatient treatment are available and, depending on the nature and severity of your case, admission into a hospital ward directly from the clinic or through hospital A&E department might be necessary.

It is important that parents and significant caregivers take part in the treatment plan that is drawn up by the doctors and therapists. Help does not stop after discharge from the hospital. The patient and his family would likely require continuing therapy and any necessary interventions at home and in school. This section lists the various types of treatments that are available to help individuals who self-harm.

10.1 SELF-MANAGEMENT SKILLS
Self-management skills includes a whole array of skills and techniques that individuals can employ to help themselves cope in the face of strong negative

emotions or great distress. These skills and techniques include stress and anxiety management, anger management, relaxation techniques, time management, social skills training and problem-solving skills. These skills are usually taught by trained counsellors and psychologists.

Anger management skills

These help individuals recognise the trigger points that arouse unpleasant emotions in them and teach them how to deal with the emotions before they become impulsive and destructive.

Social skills and assertive training

These teach individuals how to be more assertive and to say "no" to negative peer pressures and influences.

Relaxation techniques

These help individuals cope with situational stresses through the use of deep breathing exercises, guided imagery, progressive muscle relaxation as well as distractions. Meditation, listening to music, reading, writing poems, drawing, singing and other creative pursuits can sometimes allow individuals to represent their feelings through other means without harming themselves.

10.2 PSYCHOTHERAPY

Young persons who self-harm can learn how to cope with the difficult feelings that typically cause self-harm. These feelings are addressed through the use of various forms of therapy. The following are two main psychotherapies for the treatment of self-harming behaviours.

Cognitive Behavioural Therapy (CBT)

CBT encompasses two components of change—cognitive (thinking, awareness and perception) and behavioural. The cognitive approach targets and corrects erroneous thinking processes that are commonly found in individuals with low self-esteem and those suffering from anxiety disorders and depression. The behavioural approach, on the other hand, serves to modify or moderate behavioural patterns through techniques such as modelling, gradual exposure, desensitisation and response prevention.

In clinical studies on depression, children and adolescents respond to CBT with fewer symptoms of depression and anxiety. Through cognitive restructuring, behavioural modification and various skills training, the young person is more likely to have lower rates of depression, and enjoy improvements in cognitions and activity levels.

For individuals who self-harm, CBT is usually conducted one-to-one by a trained psychologist or psychiatrist. It is conducted in the clinic, which is deemed to be a safe and secure place, so that the young person feels comfortable to share his inner thoughts and feelings. Occasionally, CBT is conducted in a group format.

Dialectical Behavioural Therapy (DBT)

This is a form of therapy that is useful for individuals who self-harm repeatedly due to Borderline Personality Traits or Disorder. Individuals undergoing DBT attend both weekly individual sessions and group therapy.

DBT was pioneered by Marsha Linehan, an American psychologist. It is based on the theory that individuals who self-harm grow up in an invalidating environment and are unable to react normally to emotional stimulation because of biological factors such as underlying personality attributes and genetic risks for psychiatric conditions. These individuals do not know how to cope with sudden and intense surges of emotions. Their level of arousal goes up rapidly, peaks at a higher level than normal individuals, and takes a longer time to return to normal.

One of the basic principles of DBT is letting go of emotional suffering. DBT therefore focuses on learning to accept reality as it is. Accepting reality does not mean that the individual likes it or is willing to let it continue unchanged. It means realizing that the basic facts of life still remain even if one dislikes it. The aims of DBT are to:

- reduce high-risk suicidal behaviours,
- reduce behaviours that interfere with quality of life and post-traumatic responses such as recurrent flashbacks and avoidant behaviours,
- enhance self-respect,
- help individuals acquire acceptable behavioural skills.

DBT also explores the pros and cons of tolerating distress and in doing so, helps the individual make a decision not to harm himself. It also advocates taking measures to reduce vulnerability to negative emotions so that one is less likely to be overwhelmed by emotions. These measures include taking care of one's basic needs of nutrition and self-care (taking care of one's daily routines and hygiene), and getting enough sleep.

10.3 OTHER PSYCHOTHERAPIES

Psychodynamic Therapy

This is a form of psychotherapy developed by Sigmund Freud, the "father of psychoanalysis". Believing that one's childhood has a direct effect on the person's emotional and mental health, Freud used interviewing methods to retrace and relive the child's emotional life from early infancy. Some individuals who self-harm may need more in-depth therapy to explore deeper issues such as sexual abuse and trauma that date back to early childhood.

Interpersonal Therapy-Adolescent (IPT-A)

This form of therapy takes place in an individual or a group setting. There is two-sided commentary by both the therapist and individual(s). There is a lot of reiteration and paraphrasing of statements, reflecting on doubts and confusion, answering enquiries and offering of supportive statements. IPT-A is beneficial for adolescents whose depression primarily arises from interpersonal relationship problems, role transitions and conflicts, grief and social skills deficits.

Rational-Emotive Therapy

The concept behind Rational-Emotive Therapy is that thoughts control feelings. Individuals are thus taught how to rethink their situations and learn how to control negative feelings. Using the ABC (Antecedent-Behaviour-Consequence) approach, self-harmers are taught to:

- examine and study their beliefs, feelings and actions,
- come up with positive counter-statements to dispute and challenge their wrong beliefs,
- set realistic goals,
- put up constructive options,
- review the results when the option is put into practice.

10.4 FAMILY THERAPY

Many individuals who self-harm come from chaotic, dysfunctional or abusive family backgrounds, and have suffered emotional, physical or sexual abuse. These traumas are not easily forgotten and usually leave an indelible mark in a person's psyche. Family violence, parental break-up, divorce and custody issues can have a detrimental emotional impact on these individuals. Therefore, family work involving both the self-harmer and his family members needs to be done as the child or young person still lives within the family unit. A trained family therapist is required to:

- act as a facilitator during therapy,
- reflect on the observations made,
- highlight the necessary points and conclusions so that each family member can see their contribution to the problem.

The intention of family therapy is to bring about a change in the attitudes of each family member and propel each member to think about what he or she can do about the problem. Very rarely would self-harmers require alternative care arrangements in residential homes or hostels.

10.5 PHARMACOLOGICAL TREATMENT

Individuals who have psychiatric conditions such as depression, post-traumatic stress disorder and severe anxiety may need to take medications to ease the depression, help stabilise their moods and calm anxiety. New drugs that target specific symptoms are now available. These drugs are generally better tolerated and include minor tranquillisers, anti-depressants and mood stabilisers. A child psychiatrist would be able to prescribe the appropriate medications for those who need them.

Since low serotonin levels are implicated in self-harm behaviours, medication such as Selective Serotonin Re-uptake Inhibitors (SSRIs) that corrects this deficit are often used. These newer generation medications are known for their efficacy, fewer side effects and improved safety profile. Available only on prescription, these drugs include Fluoxetine (Prozac), Fluvoxamine (Faverin), Escitalopram (Lexapro), Paroxetine (Seroxat) and Sertraline (Zoloft). Older-generation medications such as Tricyclic Antidepressants (TCA) and Monoamine Oxidase Inhibitors (MAOIs) tend to have more side effects such as nausea, drowsiness and giddiness, and may even lead to blood pressure changes and heart problems, especially if taken in excessive doses. TCAs and MAOIs can be lethal during overdoses.

10.6 HOSPITALISATION

Hospitalisation might be necessary if the individual is in danger of seriously harming himself repeatedly, planning to attempt suicide, or if his family is not available, not supportive or too disruptive for proper care and supervision to take place. Hospitalisation offers several advantages, namely:

- a safe and secure environment,
- the opportunity to engage the person in therapy,
- time for the therapist to evaluate the person and his family situation,
- a brief respite for family members who are emotionally and physically exhausted from all the constant vigilance and worry.

Individuals who are not treated in hospitals can rely on an extensive support system. This includes frequent family therapy sessions, intensive case management, regular phone contacts to check on progress, networking with other counselling and mental health agencies, and mobilising support from the child's extended families, teachers and friends.

10.7 WHERE CAN I GO FOR HELP?

At any time when you need help or advice about handling young persons with self-harm tendencies, you can speak to trained volunteers and staff in nationwide crisis centres and telephone hotlines. (A list is provided at the end of the book.)

A telephone helpline is also a good means to reach out to young people who refuse to talk about their problems with their parents or are too shy to see a counsellor. They may be more amenable to talk and establish a relationship with a counsellor over the telephone as an anonymous caller. On assessing the severity of the problem, the telephone counsellor can direct the caller to the appropriate services. The staff who run these hotlines are trained, sensitive and sympathetic.

In schools, counsellors can be the first-line professional to help assess and counsel the student who self-harms. Should the student's condition be more complex or severe, school counsellors can seek professional assistance from REACH (Response, Early Intervention and Assessment in Community Mental Health), a community-based program led by IMH, NUHS and KKH. It has been

CASE STUDY

On one occasion, Amy had to be admitted to hospital after she had cut herself too deeply. The triggers for her self-harm were due to a culmination of factors such as strained relationship with her parents, recent arguments with her boyfriend and being bullied in school.

A psychiatrist was assigned to see her. In her sessions with the psychiatrist, Amy was encouraged to relate her feelings and disappointments in her life. Her therapist also acknowledged her negative feelings and sense of loss. She joined a group of young teenagers who had self-harmed and learnt that her problem was not unique. She felt relieved and was also keen to learn how others overcame their self-harm behaviours.

Besides individual counselling and Cognitive Behavioural Therapy, Amy also learnt healthier and adaptive ways of coping with frustration and stress. She did not require any form of medication. Upon discharge, the temptation to cut herself sometimes arose as she faced several challenges in her daily life. But she managed to postpone her cutting by distracting herself with other activities. She was very happy when she managed to stop cutting herself for two whole weeks. Today, Amy has resumed her studies and is coping well. However, the scars on her arms will never go away.

set up since 2009 to support and assist school counsellors in identifying and managing students with mental health problems. Besides assessments, REACH can also perform interventions for students in their schools or in their homes, thus bringing mental health care closer to those who need them. In partnership with the ministry of education, voluntary welfare organisations and select group of general practitioners, REACH service is available now for all public schools from primary schools to junior colleges, and including all special schools.

There are also walk-in centres for youths with emotional difficulties such as CHAT (Community Health Assessment Team), a community programme set up by IMH and sited within the SCAPE building in downtown Orchard. Youths aged 16 years and above could just walk in and seek a consult. After preliminary assessment and triage by a trained counsellor, they would be referred to the appropriate agency for best possible help.

Joining a self-help or support group for persons who self-harm and for their families can be very therapeutic when they realise that their problems are not unique to themselves. Sharing experiences in a group offers sufferers and their families a medium to express their joys and pains. In the safe and warm environment that support groups provide, many people are allowed to revisit their traumatic past experiences or difficult feelings. They also learn from each other ways to cope with their emotions in a more adaptive and meaningful way. The doctor or therapist who attends to your child can put you in touch with these support groups.

Certainly, there is a chance that some self-harmers might share ideas about how to go about hurting themselves. However, this can be avoided by having trained facilitators in the group.

> I would rather talk to somebody now than to harm myself.
> And if I know that they are not going to judge me
> for what I am, that would help.
> — Amy

PREVENTING SELF-HARM BEHAVIOURS

PART 11

Preventing self-harm from occurring is a multifaceted approach involving parents, teachers and the community. There are some strategies that can help prevent self-harm from occurring in young persons. While the effectiveness of some of these strategies is being debated, it seems likely that the most promising approaches are those that:

- focus on preventing depressive disorders,
- resolve the root causes of depressive disorders (these include socio-economic problems, disruptive or abusive relationships),
- improve life skills through educational programmes.

11.1 HOW CAN I PREVENT SELF-HARM BEHAVIOURS FROM DEVELOPING IN MY CHILD?

You can start by educating yourself about self-harm in general. There are many books and Internet websites that offer advice and information about self-harm behaviours. Recognising the signs of depression and self-harm and intervening early can help prevent self-harm behaviours from developing and taking root.

11.2 I THINK MY CHILD IS INJURING HIMSELF. WHAT SHOULD I DO?

If you detect something is amiss in your child, do not overreact. Remain calm and make yourself available to him. Ask him privately about the things that could be bothering him. State your concerns and what you have noticed about his behaviour that worries you. If you strongly suspect that self-harm is occurring, broach the topic slowly and tactfully. Remember, talking about self-harm does not increase self-harm behaviour. Your child might feel relieved knowing that someone has noticed his moods, and is willing to listen to him and not pass judgment on him.

You should also encourage your child to participate in recreational activities and sports. These are therapeutic and help release tension. They also instill a sense of pride and belonging to a group which can raise the child's self-esteem. Life routines, including fun activities within the family, should still carry on as usual. If your family practices a religion, use the teachings and activities to help your child develop a sense of inner peace. Make sure you meet your child's basic needs for love, companionship and security so that he does not feel alone and unloved.

Finally, get to know your child's friends as they are often the first to notice early warning signs and self-destructive symptoms. Once you establish a good relationship with his friends, they are more likely to come to you with their concerns.

11.3 WHAT CAN SCHOOLS DO TO PREVENT SELF-HARM?

One promising prevention strategy is to promote overall mental health among school children. Mental health promotion programmes in schools typically try to increase students' awareness of the various problems and their signs and symptoms, provide knowledge about the behavioural characteristics of teens at risk, and describe available treatment or counseling resources.

Organise workshops on children mental health for teachers

Workshops that are led by child psychiatrists and psychologists can help equip teachers with basic information and counselling skills to handle young people with problems, including self-harm behaviours.

Organise talks for students

Students will benefit from talks on stress and anxiety management, common adolescent problems and parent-child issues. These could be led by mental health professionals, counselors as well as psychologists from the Ministry of Education.

Establish procedures

Teachers and school counsellors should establish standard procedures to handle students who self-harm. They should also learn how to approach the issue sensitively and in a confidential manner so as to instill a sense of trust and safety.

Engage parents

It is important to keep the student's parents informed about their child. This engagement should begin early in the student's counseling process. With parental agreement, schools can refer students directly to the REACH programme where their cases are triaged and assessed. If necessary, they are then referred to either one of the two Child Guidance Clinics or to the child psychiatric clinics in NUHS and KKH. Thankfully, majority of self-harm cases require only outpatient therapy and treatment. Only the very serious cases of self-harming require admission to hospitals with child psychiatric services so as to ensure the safety of the child. It is important to clarify at this point that for individuals with high suicide risk, IMH remains the only admitting hospital as it is a place of safety for suicidal patients.

11.4 WHO ARE THE CHILDREN AT RISK? HOW CAN WE IDENTIFY THEM SO THAT THEY GET THE SUPPORT THEY NEED?

One positive way of preventing self-harm behaviours from developing is to identify children and young persons who come from high-risk families. Early detection is an important step as it allows teachers and healthcare professionals to take proactive measures against self-harm. Some markers that characterise a high-risk family include:

- marital discord between parents,
- mental illness in parents (particularly depression),
- family history of self-harm or suicide,
- dysfunctional and chaotic family structure and dynamics (divorce, neglect, violence and abuse),
- over-controlling and over-critical parenting styles,
- adverse living conditions and environment (poor economic status, lack of basic daily provisions or over-crowding).

The markers that characterise a high-risk individual are:
- history of physical and sexual abuse or emotional abuse in childhood,
- poor relationship with parents,
- few friends,
- discrimination by peers for being different, (quiet and timid disposition, physical handicaps and psychiatric conditions).

There are also identifiable stressors which could give rise to emotional or psychological problems and therefore should be identified early, such as:
- issues dealing with growing up, such as demands for independence,
- boy-girl relationship problems, including unwanted pregnancies,
- bullying in school,
- conflicting or intense sexual feelings,
- identity crisis (conflict between a person's wishes or desires against the expectations of others),
- problems with peers and friends,
- bereavement and loss of loved ones,
- pressures of schoolwork or work,
- substance abuse and related problems.

WHAT IS THE PROGNOSIS
FOR SELF-HARMERS?

PART 12

The natural course of self-harm is long and tumultuous for those who are chronic sufferers. This is attributed to the high degree of emotional disturbance and irresolution of the core problems that these sufferers endure. Furthermore, self-harm behaviours may wax and wane over time according to the occurrences of stresses in a young person's life. Many individuals continue to self-harm until early adulthood.

However, as situations improve and with maturity of thought and better control of impulses, self-harm behaviours do generally improve over time in terms of their severity and frequency.

Early intervention and appropriate referral to psychological services tend to bring about a better outcome. As a whole, the prognosis is fairly optimistic with up to 40 per cent of self-harmers eventually reducing or stopping their self-harm behaviours. For those who stop self-harm on their own, an improved self-esteem seems to be a significant factor. Other important contributing factors for improvement include:

- working through one's feelings from the past,
- growing up and maturing thoughts,
- better and more effective communication,
- stable and supportive environment.

❝ When I look back to the time when I used to hurt myself a lot, I feel foolish. But it taught me to be strong and not give up. The idea of cutting myself was tempting, but the feeling of being a master of my own actions was even greater. Now that I'm older, I've never looked back since. I'm as normal as anyone else. I have a beautiful family now. ❞

— a survivor

USEFUL RESOURCES

Journal Articles

Ho, B.K.W. and Kua, E.H. (1998). "Parasuicide: a Singapore perspective" in *Ethnicity and Health*, 3: 255-263.

International Society for the Study of Self-Injury. (2007). *Definitional Issues Surrounding Our Understanding of Self-injury.* Conference proceedings from the annual meeting.

Loh, C.; Teo Y.W. and Lim, L. (2013). "Deliberate Self-harm in Adolescent Psychiatric Outpatients in Singapore: Prevalence and Associated Risk Factors" in *Singapore Medical Journal* 54(9), pp 491–495.

Rodham, K. and Hawton, K. (2009). "Epidemiology and Phenomenology of Nonsuicidal Self-injury" in M.K. Nock (Ed.), *Understanding Nonsuicidal Self-injury: Origins, Assessment and Treatment*. Washington DC: American Psychological Association, pp 37–62.

Solomon, Y. and Farrand, J. (1996). "'Why Don't You Do It Properly?': Young Women Who Self-injure" in *Journal of Adolescence* 19(2), pp 111–119.

Tay, A.T.S. and Cheng, S.E.T. (2014). *Socio-demographic and Clinical Profile of Self-harm Patients in a General Hospital.* XVI World Congress of Psychiatry, Madrid.

Tuisku, V.; Pelkonen, M.; Kiviruusu, O.; Karlsson, L.; Ruuttu, T. and Marttunen, M. (2009). "Factors Associated with Deliberate Self-harm Behaviour Among Depressed Adolescent Outpatients" in *Journal of Adolescence* 32(5), pp 1125–1136.

Books

Alderman, T. *The Scarred Soul: Understanding and Ending Self-inflicted Violence.* New Harbinger Publications, 1997.

Bywaters, P. and Rolfe, A. *Look Beyond The Scars: Understanding and Responding to Self-injury and Self-harm.* NCH (UK-based children's charity organisation), 2002. Text available online in pdf format from www.nch.org.uk

Chia, B.H. *Suicidal Behaviour in Singapore*. Tokyo SEAMIC, 1981.

Cronkite, K. *On the Edge of Darkness: Conversations about Conquering Depression.* Delta Control and Prevention, National Center for Injury Prevention and Control, 1995.

Favazza, A.R. *Bodies Under Siege: Self-Mutilation in Culture and Society.* The John Hopkins University Press, 3rd edition, 2011.

Kreisman, J. and Strauss, H. *I Hate You: Don't Leave Me.* Avon Press, 1989.

Klonsky, E. David; Muehlenkamp, Jennifer J.; Lewis, Stephen P.; and Walsh, Barent. *Nonsuicidal Self-Injury*, in the series "Advances in Psychotherapy, Evidence Based Practice". Hogrefe Publishing, 2011.

Miller, D. *Women Who Hurt Themselves: A Book of Hope and Understanding*. Basic Books, 2005.

Nixon, Mary K. and Heath, Nancy L. (editors). *Self-Injury in Youth: The Essential Guide to Assessment and Intervention*. Routledge, 2008.

Shapiro, Lawrence E. *Stopping the Pain: A Workbook for Teens Who Cut and Self Injure.* Instant Help, 2008.

Websites

Ministry of Social and Family Development
www.msf.gov.sg

Cornell Research Program on Self-Injurious Behaviours (CRPSIB)
www.selfinjury.bctr.cornell.edu/

National Self-harm Network (UK)
www.nshn.co.uk/index.html

Self-Injury Foundation
www.selfinjuryfoundation.org/

YoungMinds
www.youngminds.org.uk

Telephone Hotlines

SOS Helpline
Tel: 1800-2214444
24-hour service offering confidential emotional support
and general counselling to individuals in crisis

Tinkle Friend
Tel: 1800-2744788
Helpline for children run by the Singapore Children's Society

National Family Service Centre
Tel: 1800-8380100
Automated hotline number to direct callers to their nearest neighbourhood family service
centres. Service provided by National Council of Social Services (NCSS).

Parentline
Tel: 62898811
Hotline number for parents with young and teenage children. Run by Covenant Family
Service Centre. Available from 9 am to 5 pm, Mondays to Fridays.

Child and adolescent psychiatry clinics in public and restructured hospitals

Child Guidance Clinic
CGC@Health Promotion Board Building
3 Second Hospital Avenue Singapore 168937

CGC@Sunrise Wing
Institute of Mental Health
10 Buangkok View Singapore 539747
Tel: 6389 2000 (mainline), 6389 2200 (appointment line),
    6389 2222 (24-hour Mental Health Helpline)
    www.imh.com.sg

Changi General Hospital (adolescent psychiatry only)
Tel: 6788 8833 (mainline), 6850 3333 (appointment line)
www.cgh.com.sg

KK Women's and Children's Hospital (internal referrals only)
Tel: 6225 5554 (mainline)
www.kkh.com.sg

Khoo Teck Phuat Hospital
Tel: 6555 8000 (mainline), 6555 8828 (appointment line)
https://www.ktph.com.sg

National University Hospital Systems
Tel: 6779 5555 (mainline), 6772 2002 (appointment line)
www.nuhs.edu.sg/

Child and adolescent psychiatric services in private hospitals
Adam Road Medical Centre
Camden Medical Centre
Gleneagles Hospital
Mt Elizabeth—Charter Behavioural Health Services
Mount Elizabeth Hospital

ABOUT THE AUTHOR

Dr Ong Say How graduated from the National University of Singapore with a Masters in Psychiatry in 1999 and obtained his Graduate Diploma in Psychotherapy in 2002. After completing his Research Fellowship in Columbia University and New York State Psychiatric Institute (NYSPI) in 2005, he has been deeply engaged in outpatient services for children and adolescents with psychological problems and has conducted research work in mood disorders, schizophrenia, cyberaddiction and Attention Deficit Hyperactivity Disorder (ADHD). Recently conferred an Adjunct Assistant Professor by Yong Loo Lin School of Medicine, National University of Singapore (NUS), Dr Ong is also a core faculty member of the National Psychiatric Residency Program and serves as a Clinical Teacher of DUKE-NUS Graduate Medical School.

Dr Ong has chosen to specialise in the field of child and adolescent psychiatry because of his natural rapport and easy connection with young children and teenagers. He believes that every child and teen deserves a voice of their own amidst the multitude of challenges that they face in the real world today.

Having special interest in public education, Dr Ong has spoken widely in the local TV and radio media and in schools. He has also contributed articles regarding mental health issues in the young for several books and magazines. In 2002, he wrote a short story "Nick's In Trouble Again" about managing misconduct in children and co-authored several other books on child and adolescent mental health.

Currently practicing at IMH's Child Guidance Clinic located at Health Promotion Board, Dr Ong manages a whole range of childhood emotional and psychological conditions ranging from Anxiety, Depression, ADHD, Autism Spectrum Disorders to Early Psychosis. He is also a visiting consultant at KK Women's & Children's Hospital and heads its Child & Adolescent Mental Wellness Service.